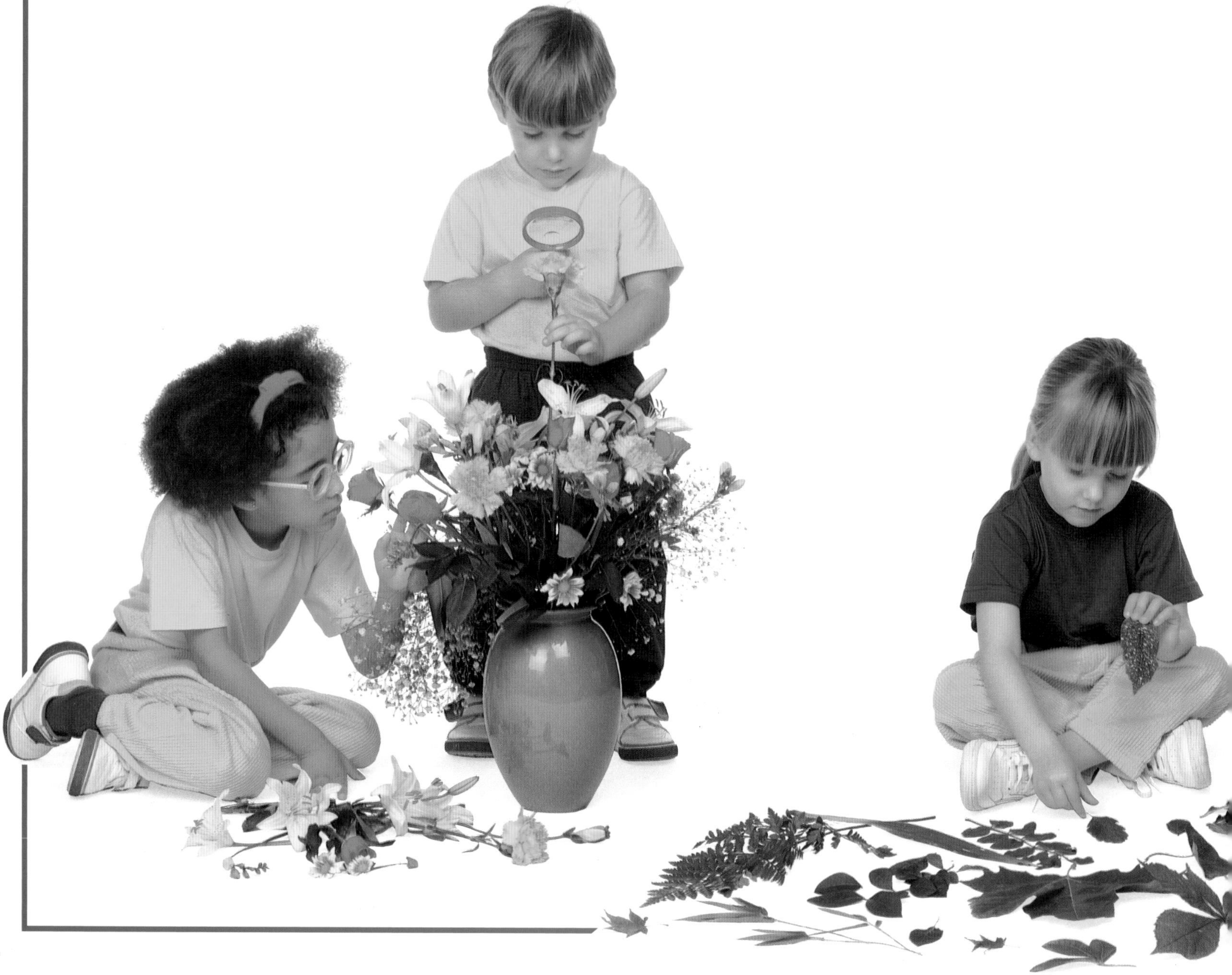

◆ LET'S EXPLORE SCIENCE ◍

Living Things

▲ David Evans and Claudette Williams ☐

DORLING KINDERSLEY EDUCATION
London • New York • Stuttgart

A DORLING KINDERSLEY BOOK

Project Editor Stella Love
Art Editor Sara Nunan
Designer Cheryl Telfer
Managing Editor Jane Yorke
Managing Art Editor Chris Scollen
Production Jayne Wood
Photography by Daniel Pangbourne

This is a Dorling Kindersley Education edition, 1993
0 9 8 7 6 5 4 3 2 1

First published in the United States by
Dorling Kindersley, Inc., 232 Madison Avenue
New York, 1993

Library of Congress Cataloging-in-Publication Data

Evans, David, 1937-
    Living things / by David Evans and Claudette Williams. -- 1st American ed.
      p.   cm. -- (Let's explore science)
    Includes index.
    Summary: Simple experiments explore the habitats, growth, and nature of living things.
    ISBN 1-56458-345-7 (trade edition)
    ISBN 0-7516-4914-7 (school edition)
    1. Biology--Experiments--Juvenile literature. 2. Biology--Fieldwork--Juvenile literature.
[1. Biology--Experiments. 2. Experiments.]
I. Williams, Claudette. II. Title. III. Series.
QH316.5E915 1993
574'.072--dc20   93-7073
                                                     CIP
                                                     AC

Manufactured in Belgium

Dorling Kindersley would like to thank the following for their help in producing
this book: Paul Bricknell; Jane Burton; Peter Chadwick; Gordon Clayton;
Philip Dowell; Michael Dunning; Steve Gorton; Frank Greenaway; Colin Keates;
Dave King; Bob Langrish; Cyril Laubscher; Stephen Oliver; Susanna Price;
Steve Shot; James Stevenson; Kim Taylor; and Jerry Young
(for additional photography); Coral Mula (for safety symbol artwork);
Mark Richards (for jacket design); Animal Ark; Rocky Road Productions Ltd.;
Susan Noyce and Adrian Talbot; and the Franklin Delano Roosevelt School, London.
Dorling Kindersley would also like to give special thanks to the following for appearing
in this book: Natalie Agada; Marc Belsey; Hannah Capleton; Steven Cawley;
Gregory Coleman; Pandora Dickey; Adam Lewis; Tony Locke; Rachel Malicki;
Kim Ng; Tanya Pham; Daniel Sach; and Anthony Singh.

Contents

Note to parents and teachers

Young children are forever asking questions about the things they see, touch, hear, smell, and taste. The **Let's Explore Science** series aims to foster children's natural curiosity and encourages them to use their senses to find out about science. Each book features a variety of experiments based on one topic, which draw on a young child's everyday experiences. By investigating familiar activities, such as bouncing a ball, making cookies, or clapping hands, young children will learn that science plays an important part in the world around them.

Investigative approach

Young children can only begin to understand science if they are stimulated to think and to find out for themselves. For these reasons, an open-ended questioning approach is used in the **Let's Explore Science** books and, wherever possible, results of experiments are not shown. Children are encouraged to make their own scientific discoveries, and to interpret them according to their own ideas. This investigative approach to learning makes science exciting and not just about acquiring "facts." This way of learning will assist children in many areas of their education.

Using the books

Before starting an experiment, check the text and pictures to ensure that you have gathered any necessary equipment. Allow children to help in this process and to suggest alternative materials to use. Once ready, it is important to let children decide how to carry out the experiment and what the result means to them. You can help by asking questions, such as, "What do you think will happen?" or "What did you do?"

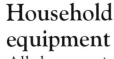

Household equipment

All the experiments can be carried out easily at home. In most cases, inexpensive household objects and materials are used.

Guide to experiments

The *Guide to experiments* on pages 28-29 is intended to help parents, teachers, or helpers using this book with children. It gives an outline of the scientific principles underlying the experiments, includes useful tips for carrying out the activities, suggests alternative equipment to use, and additional activities to try.

Safe experimenting

This symbol appears next to experiments where children may require adult supervision or assistance, such as, when they are heating things or using sharp tools.

About this book

The experiments in **Living Things** lead children to examine a wide variety of plants and animals and to explore life processes. By collecting and planting seeds, studying small animals, and comparing species, children will begin to understand that:

- basic life processes, such as breathing, are common to humans and other animals;

- living things grow and change, and the variety of living things, including both animal and plant life, is immense;

- living things are found in different places and each species favors a type of habitat;

- careful observation is required to make accurate comparisons and find similarities and differences between living things;

- if animals are to survive, either in the wild or in captivity, we need to consider their welfare and be sensitive to their needs.

With your help, young children will enjoy exploring the world of science and discover that finding out is fun.

David Evans and
Claudette Williams

What is alive?

Look at things around you, in your home, or when you are outside. How do you know if something is alive?

Wear gloves and be careful not to harm living things when you handle them.

Living things
Which of the things shown here are alive? Which things are nonliving?

Which things were once part of a living thing?

Can you tell which living things they came from?

Breathing things
What things
can you see
breathing?
Where does
the air go
in and
come out?

Growing things
What things grow
and are alive?

Moving things
What things move
and are alive?

11

Where do things live?

Where can you find living things? What kinds of places can you think of in which to look?

At home
How many living things can you find in your home?

On the farm or in the wild
Can you make or cut out pictures of farm animals and wild animals? Can you make posters with the pictures?

On the shoreline
Which animals live on the shoreline? Are they easy to find?

In a park or backyard
What things live in your backyard? Do they live in the grass, in trees, in the soil, or under stones?

In a pond
What things can you find living in a pond? Do they live on the surface or in the water?

Wash your hands after touching pond water.

How many different trees and plants can you find?

Can you collect living things?

Gently collect some living things, but be careful not to harm them.

Can you catch things with a sieve, a colander, or a spoon?

Fishing net
Can you use a net to catch some animals that live in water? Can you gently put them into a bucket of water?

Always put animals back where you found them.

Collecting bottle

Can you make a collecting bottle like this? Ask an adult to cut the top off a plastic bottle for you.

tape

plastic bottle

air holes

cover

rubber band

jar

Collecting jars

Find some plastic jars to use for collecting things. Cut out muslin or paper covers and fix them in place with rubber bands.

Catching tub

What animals might you catch if you leave a tub in some soil? Balance a cover on two stones, over the tub, to keep the rain out.

How will you care for the animals you collect?

Can you study living things?

What can you find out
about snails and wood lice?

Snail's head
What will happen
if you gently touch
a snail on its head?

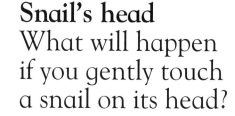

Snail home
Can you make a snail home?
Put some stones and damp
soil into a tank. Make some
air holes in the lid and put
something heavy on top
to keep the snails from
escaping.

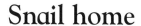

Snail food
Do snails prefer to eat
cabbage or lettuce?

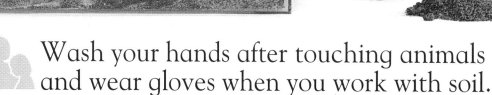

Wash your hands after touching animals
and wear gloves when you work with soil.

16

Wood lice home
Can you find some wood lice?
Put them into a box of soil.
What will the wood lice
do if you cover half of
the box?

Studying animals
Look closely
at some animals. Can you
draw or write about
what you see?

Wet soil
Do wood lice
prefer wet
soil or dry
soil?

Eyes
Do wood lice
have eyes?

What are living things like?

Can you find lots of different animals and plants to look at?

Legs
How many legs do animals have? Do all animals move in the same way?

Head and body
Do all animals have a head? What shapes and colors are their bodies?

Skin
What sort of skin do animals have? Is it rough or smooth?

Flowers

Do all flowers
have petals?
Do all flowers
smell the same?

Plants

Do all plants have
roots, leaves, and
a stem?

bud

flower

leaves

stem

roots

Leaves

How many types of leaves
can you find? Can you sort
them into groups?

Do not pick
wildflowers.

Are all plants the same?

Where do fruits and vegetables come from? Where do you find seeds?

Fruits

Ask an adult to help you cut some fruits in half. What do they look like inside? Are they all the same?

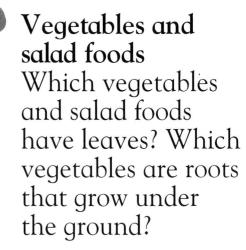

Trees
What kinds of trees grow where you live? What do they look like in winter?

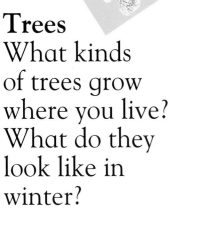

Vegetables and salad foods
Which vegetables and salad foods have leaves? Which vegetables are roots that grow under the ground?

Plants without flowers

How are these plants different from one another? Can you find other plants without flowers?

conifer

fern

seaweed

moss

Flowers

Can you press flowers with a sheet of construction paper and a pile of books? What will the flowers look like after one month?

Seeds

Can you collect some seeds from trees and plants? What is the biggest seed you can find?

How do living things grow?

How do living things grow and change?
Try these experiments to find out.

Onion bulb
How quickly
does an
onion bulb
grow in
water?

Vegetable tops
What will happen
if you leave some
vegetable tops
in a dish of
water?

Bean
Can you grow
a bean plant in
a plastic pot
lined with wet
paper towels?

Seeds
What will
happen if
you plant
some seeds
or fruit pits
in soil?

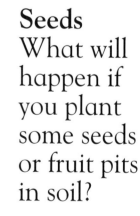

Humans

Look at photographs of yourself as a baby. How have you changed? In what ways are you different from an adult?

Caterpillar

Can you find a caterpillar on some leaves? Gently pick it up with a paintbrush. Pick some of the leaves for the caterpillar to eat.

Caterpillar home

Can you make a home for a caterpillar? Line a box with damp paper towels and put in some fresh leaves. Cover the box with muslin. Feed your caterpillar with fresh leaves every day.

After a few weeks how does the caterpillar change?

Are all animals the same?

Look at the animals on these pages. In what ways are they the same? How are they different?

Mammals

bat

sheep

piglets

Look at mammals
The animals on this page are known as mammals. Which ones have you seen?

horse

sea lion

human

dog

Do all mammals have fur or hair?

guinea pig

cat

Birds

duck

parrots

sparrow

Look at birds
How many different birds can you see in your backyard or in a park, or at the zoo?

eagle

gull

penguin

Do all birds have feathers?

heron

starling

hen

owls

Studying animals

Here are some more groups of animals to study.
Look at them carefully. Can you describe each animal?

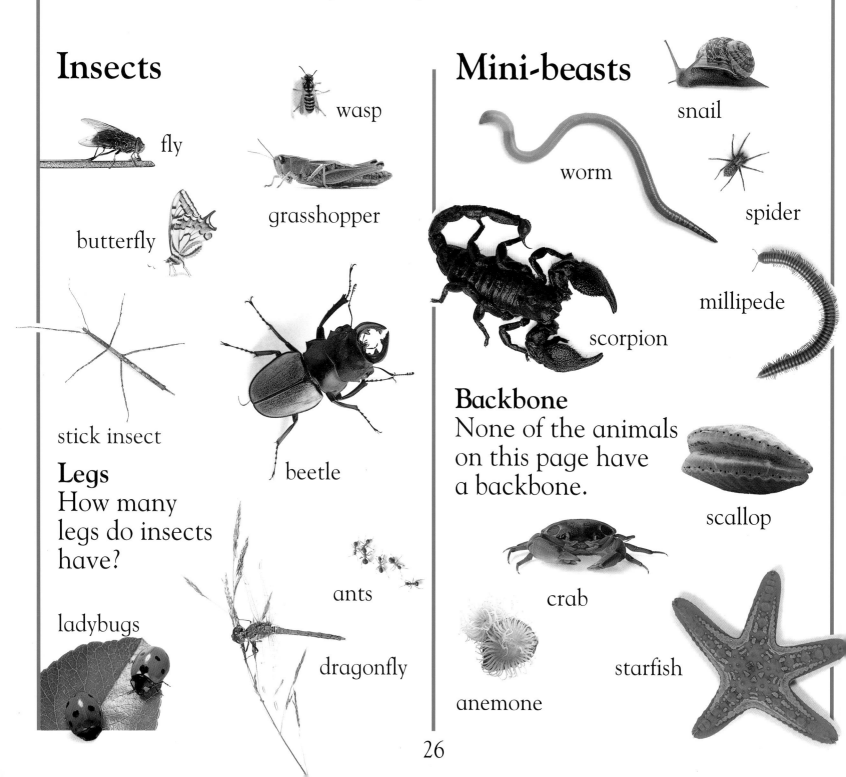

Insects

fly

wasp

grasshopper

butterfly

stick insect

beetle

Legs
How many
legs do insects
have?

ladybugs

ants

dragonfly

Mini-beasts

snail

worm

spider

scorpion

millipede

Backbone
None of the animals
on this page have
a backbone.

scallop

crab

anemone

starfish

Fish

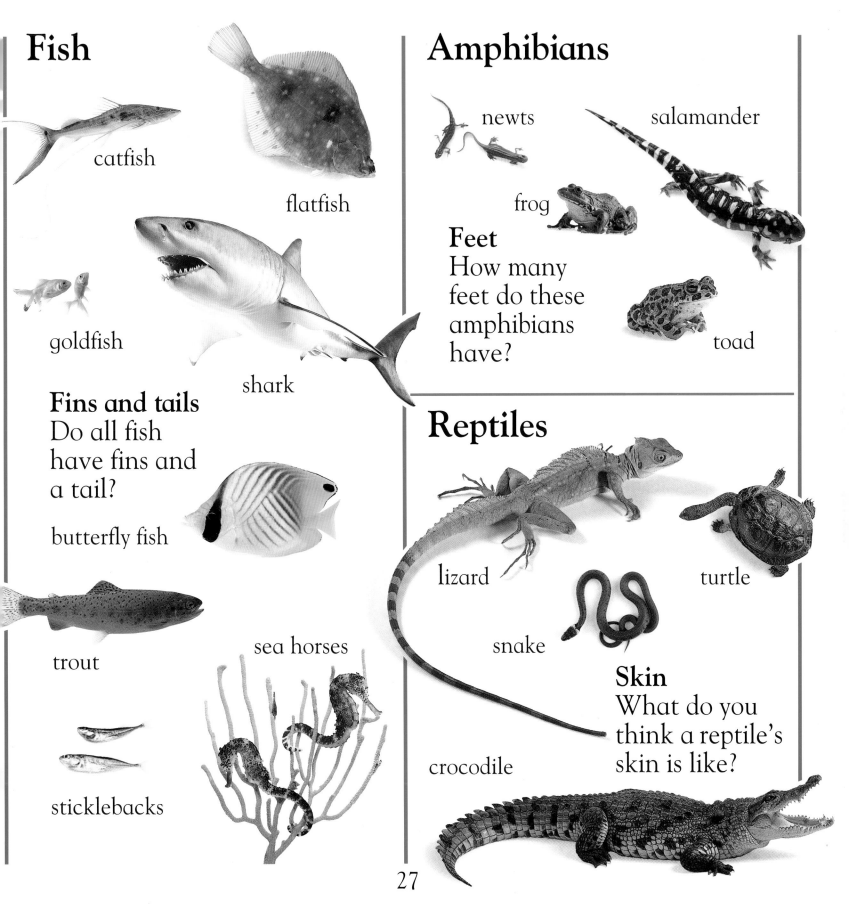

catfish

flatfish

goldfish

shark

Fins and tails
Do all fish
have fins and
a tail?

butterfly fish

trout

sea horses

sticklebacks

Amphibians

newts

salamander

frog

Feet
How many
feet do these
amphibians
have?

toad

Reptiles

lizard

snake

turtle

Skin
What do you
think a reptile's
skin is like?

crocodile

Index

Guide to experiments

The notes below briefly outline the scientific principles underlying the experiments and include suggestions for alternative equipment to use and activities to try.

What is alive? 10-11

Direct observation of living things enables children to decide what being alive means. They use the criteria of movement, breathing, and growth to judge whether things are living, dead, or have never lived at all. Further investigation could involve trying to find out if things can sense sound, taste, or smell to confirm that they are alive.

Where do things live? 12-13

Children are encouraged to explore a range of familiar habitats, to determine where living things may be found. By looking at pets and plants in the home, and then considering living things in different environments, such as, ponds and shorelines, children begin to appreciate the variety of living things.

Can you collect living things? 14-15

Here children are given ideas about how they might collect and house some small creatures to begin the process of studying living things in more detail.

Children should be reminded to think about each animal's welfare, whether it can breathe and what it will eat. After study, all animals must be released where they were found. Children should always wash their hands after handling any animals.

Can you study living things? 16-17

By working with snails and wood lice, children extend their understanding that living things need certain conditions to sustain life. The experiments are humane investigations to discover how sensitive mini-beasts are to their environment, and what foods they prefer. Similar experiments can be carried out with other small animals, such as earthworms and grasshoppers.

What are living things like? 18-19

The experiments lead children to observe the external features of a variety of animals and plants. Children should be encouraged to look for similarities and differences in the examples they study, and to describe what they see in their own words. Fur, feathers, and some plants may cause an allergic reaction in some children.

Are all plants the same? 20-21

By experimenting with fruits, vegetables, plants, flowers, and seeds, children can begin to sort them into broad groups according to their visible features. These observations can be extended by a visit to a botanical garden, garden center, or flower store. Children should be warned about the dangers of tasting seeds and berries.

How do living things grow? 22-23

The experiments show children how plants, animals, and humans grow at different rates, and change in appearance. Working with caterpillars will lead to an awareness that living things undergo a life cycle. Children should avoid species of caterpillar with long hairs because these may cause an allergic irritation.

Are all animals the same? 24-27

By studying pictures of a variety of mammals and birds, children can begin to recognize that groups of animals have physical features in common but are different in the ways that they live. The grouping, or classification, of animals continues on the following pages. By looking at similarities and differences between major groups of animals, children will begin to learn how to identify the animals they come across.